I CAN BE A

NURSE

By June Behrens

Prepared under the direction of Robert Hillerich, Ph.D.

CHILDRENS PRESS®

CHICAGO

Library of Congress Cataloging-in-Publication Data

Behrens, June.
   I can be a nurse.

  Includes index.
  Summary: Describes different kinds of nurses, their
duties, the places where they work, and how they are
trained.
  1. Nursing—Vocational guidance—Juvenile
literature. 2. Nurses—Juvenile literature.
[1. Nursing—Vocational guidance. 2. Vocational
guidance. 3. Nurses. 4. Occupations] I. Title.
RT82.B44 1986   610.73'023   85-29086
ISBN 0-516-01893-0

PICTURE DICTIONARY

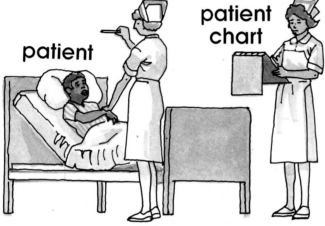

patient

patient chart

nurse

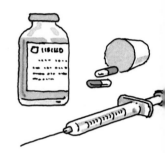

medicine

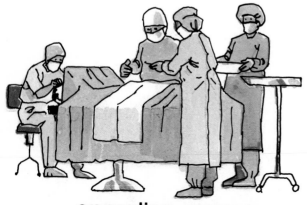

operating room

medical laboratory

nurse educator

industrial nurse

office nurse

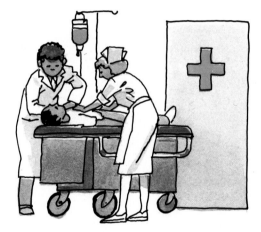

emergency room nurse

community health nurse

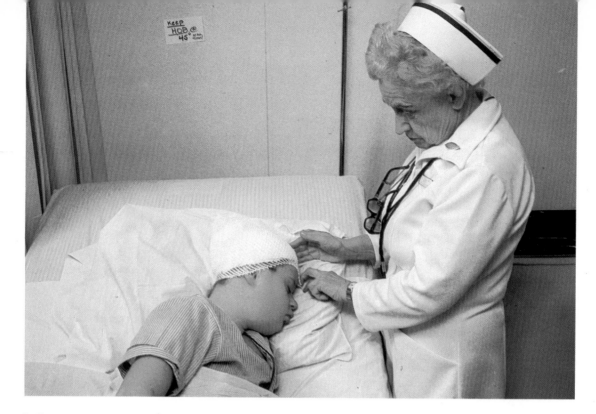

Both men and women can be nurses. Nurses care for people
who are sick or injured (above). They are also trained to
help patients whose breathing or heartbeat has stopped (below).

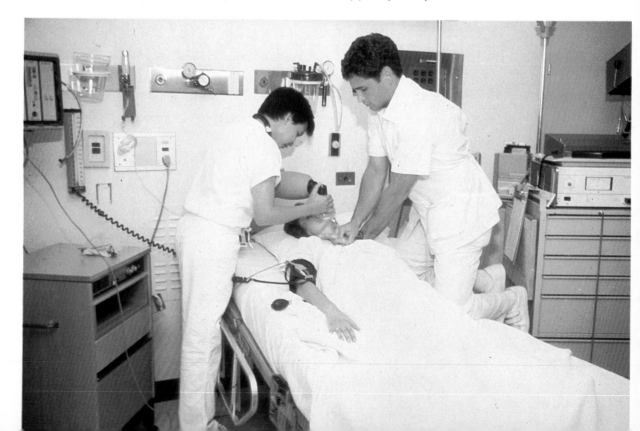

Nurses help people
who are sick and injured.
They are sometimes
called "angels of mercy."
Nurses are people who
care about people.
Would you like to be a
nurse?

nurse

Above: Nursing students studying a model of the human heart
Below: Students practice putting bandages on each other.

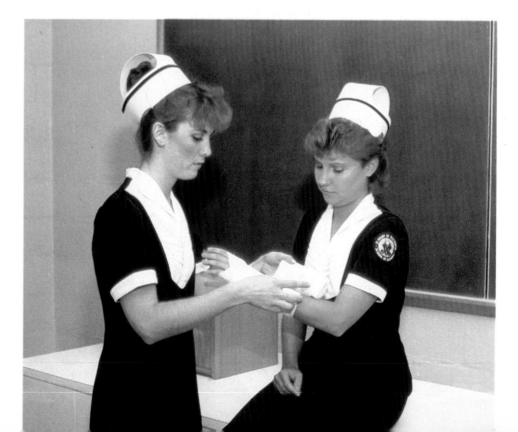

People who want to become nurses must graduate from high school. Then they must go to nursing school. There are schools for nurses in hospitals and colleges.

In school, students learn about health care. Later they become student nurses in hospitals and other health centers.

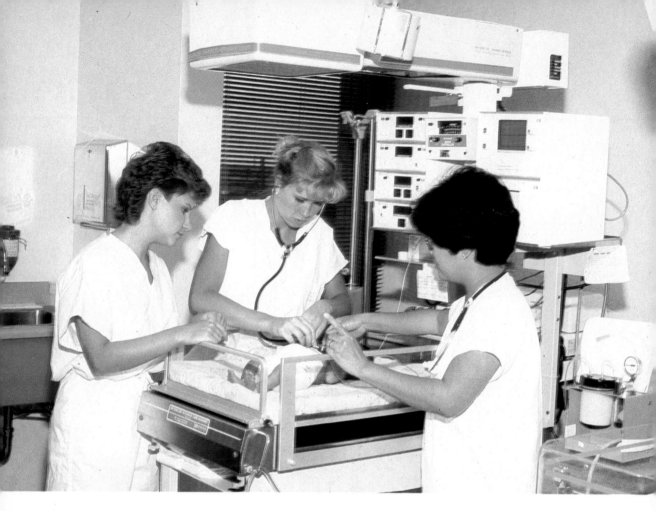

A nurse and students examine a baby in the intensive care unit.

When school is over,
the students must pass a
test. They are then
registered as nurses. R.N.
means registered nurse.

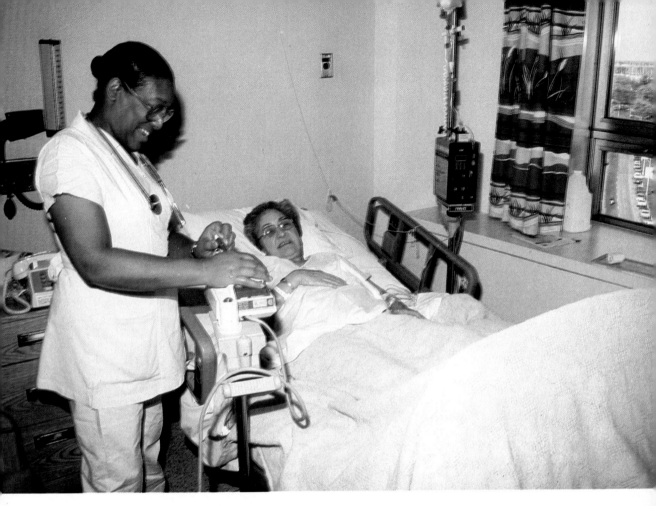

Nurses give patients tests to check on their progress.

Most registered nurses
work in hospitals. They
work with patients.
Patients are people who
need health care.

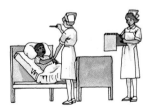

patient

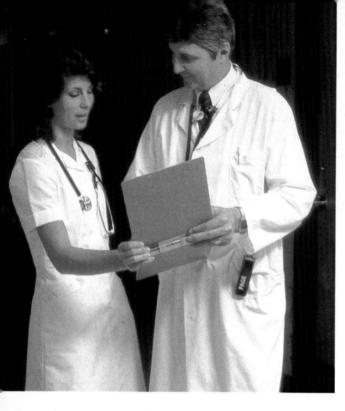

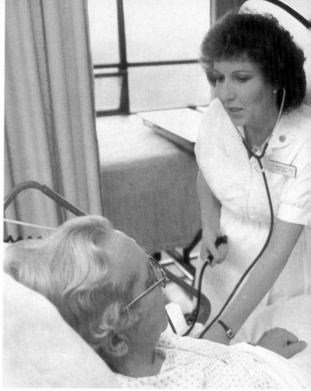

A doctor and a nurse (above left) discuss the care of one of their patients. Testing blood pressure is one way of finding out a patient's condition (above right and below).

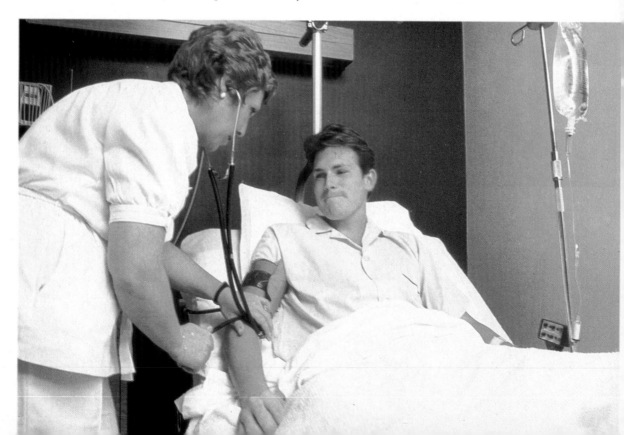

Registered nurses carry
out the orders, or
instructions, that doctors
give for patient care.
They read patient charts
and reports. Nurses give
their patients medicine
and keep records of
each patient's progress.

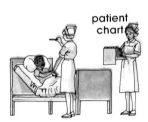

patient
chart

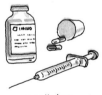

medicine

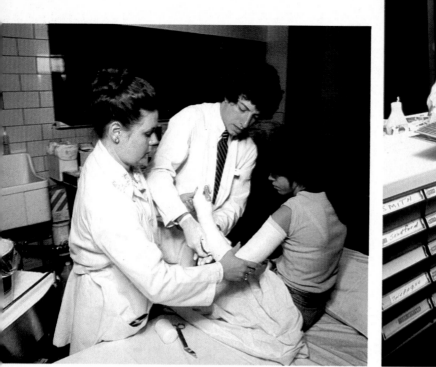

Nurse and doctor fixing a broken arm in the emergency room (left).
Nurses keep careful records on each patient (right).

Registered nurses work
with other health care
workers. They oversee the
work of practical nurses.
They direct nurse's aides
and orderlies in their
duties.

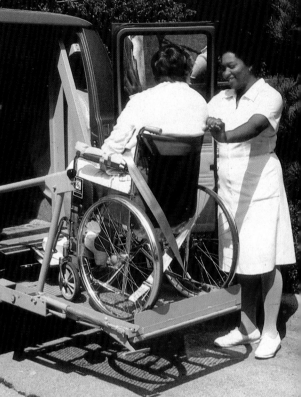

Many teenagers work as volunteers in hospitals (left).
A practical nurse (right) helps a handicapped patient get
into a van.

Practical nurses, aides,
and orderlies are part of
the health team. They
help to provide bedside
care. They serve meals
and keep patients
comfortable and clean.

An operating room nurse, or surgery nurse, applies bandages to a patient (left). A pediatrics nurse (right) takes care of children.

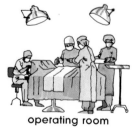

operating room

Registered nurses have special jobs in the hospital. Some work with doctors in the operating room. Others take care of new babies and children.

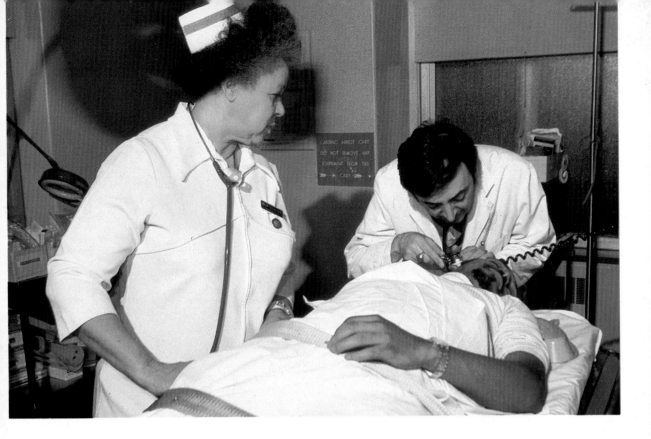

Some registered nurses work with older people or those with a special illness. Some work in a hospital's emergency room. Specialist nurses work in the medical laboratory.

emergency room nurse

medical laboratory

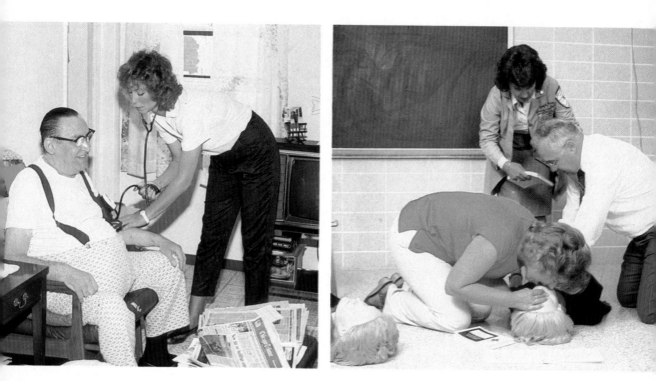

Left: A nurse taking care of a patient in his home. Right:
A nurse training people in CPR, or cardiopulmonary resuscitation.
CPR can save the life of someone whose heart has stopped beating.

community health nurse

Community health
nurses take care of
people in clinics, homes,
and schools. They tell
families about good

16

Nurses teaching schoolchildren how to care for their teeth

health care. They work
with teachers and
parents. They help with
health education in the
community.

Nurse educators are teaching nurses. They work in nursing schools and colleges. They teach student nurses. They give classes for other nurses about new ideas in nursing.

nurse educator

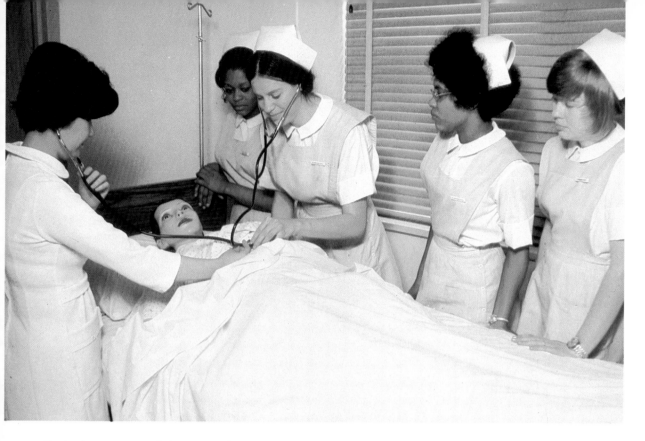

Student nurses practicing on a dummy patient (above)
and attending class (below).

Army nurses care for soldiers who have been wounded in battle.

Industrial nurses care for workers in factories and industry. They treat workers who are injured or ill. They give workers health care information. Industrial nurses help the doctor by giving health tests and shots.

industrial nurse

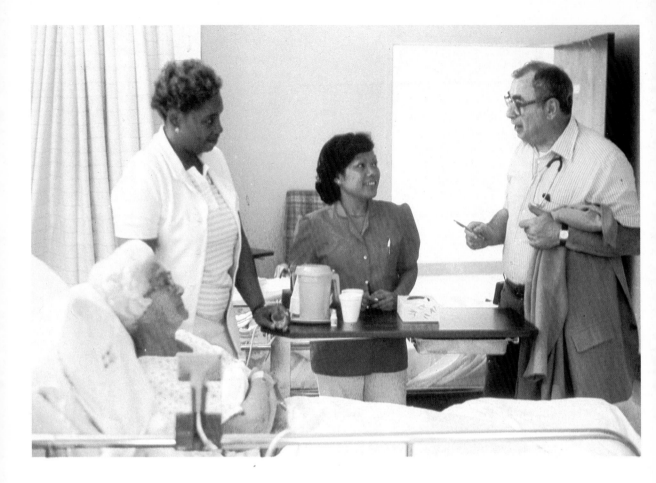

Nurses in nursing
homes care for people
who are getting over an
illness. Their patients have
many kinds of health
problems.

Above: This supervising nurse has many responsibilities.
Below: These nurses are learning about new nursing procedures.

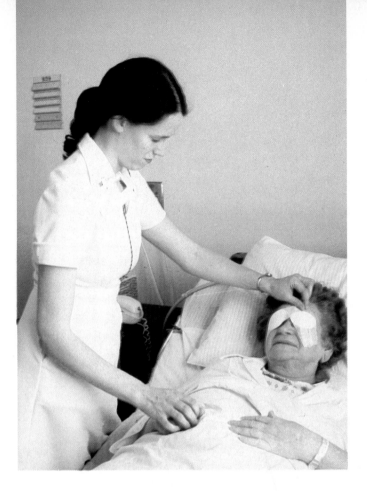

A private duty nurse looks after one patient who needs care all the time. The private duty nurse might work in the patient's home or in the hospital.

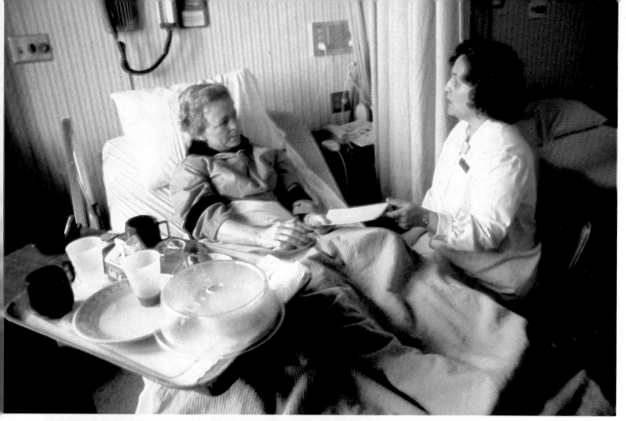

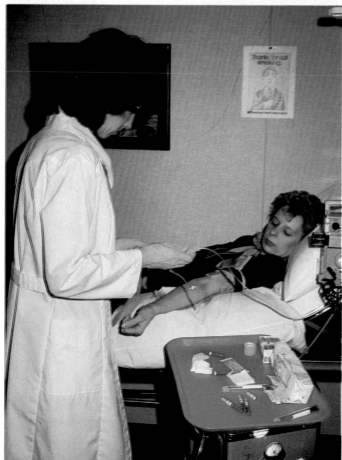

Nurses talk with their
patients (above) to help them
understand their illness and
how it is being cared for.
It is also important for
a patient to understand
what is going on in the body
as it tries to fight a disease.
The patient at left is
receiving chemotherapy as
a treatment for cancer.

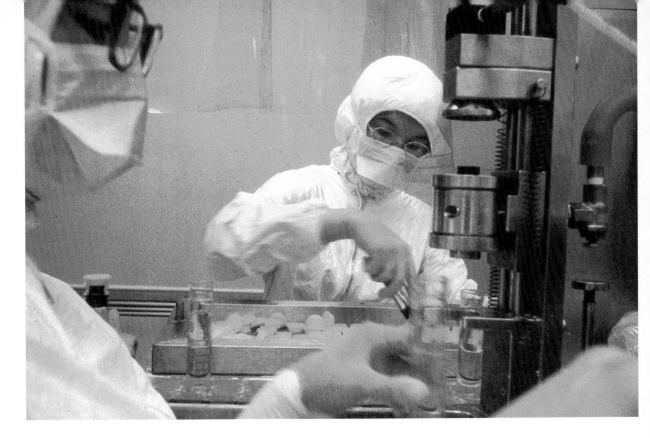

Above: Some nurses may work in a hospital laboratory.
Below: Nurses test a needle used for blood samples.

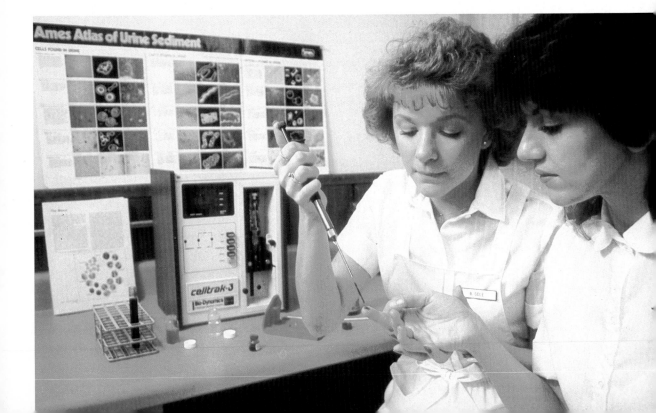

Office nurses help
doctors. They work in
private offices and
clinics. Besides nursing,
they sometimes do office
work. They may work in
the laboratory and have
many other jobs.

office nurse

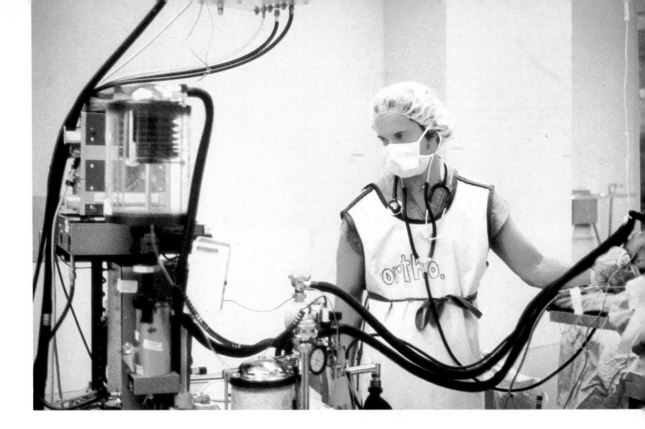

Human kindness and medical skills are what nursing is all about.

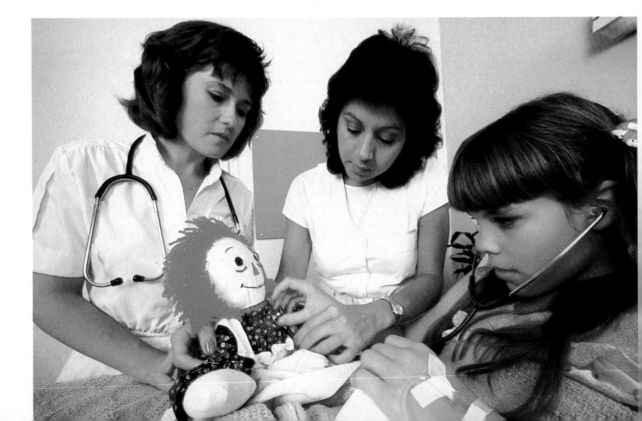

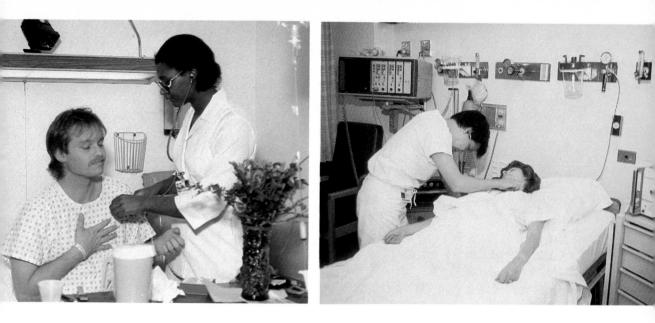

Nurses are there when
we need them. They help
patients in hospitals. They
work in the community.
They teach others. Nurses
can choose special jobs.
They can work in many
different places.

Would you like to be a
nurse?

WORDS YOU SHOULD KNOW

chart (CHAHRT)—a set of pages with information about a patient's illness, medicine, and care

clinic (KLIN • ik)—an office where people can get medical examinations and care

community (kum • YOU • nuh • tee)—a group of people who live in a certain area

educator (ED • joo • cay • tur)—a person who teaches others

emergency room (ee • MUR • jun • see ROOM)—part of a hospital where people come when they need immediate medical care

industry (IN • dus • tree)—companies doing some kind of business activity, such as manufacturing

medical laboratory (MED • ih • kil LAB • ruh • tor • ee)—a place where tests and studies are done to find out about people's diseases or medical conditions

nurse's aide (NUR • siz AYD)—a hospital worker who helps nurses with patient care

operating room (OP • uh • rayt • ing ROOM)—room in a hospital where operations, or surgery, are done

orderly (OR • der • lee)—a hospital worker who does work such as moving patients or carrying supplies

oversee (oh • ver • SEE)—to watch over or supervise

practical nurse (PRAK • tih • kil NURSS)—a nurse who has had training to care for the sick, but does not have as much training as a registered nurse

progress (PRAH • gress)—gradual improvement

registered nurse (REJ • ih • sturd NURSS)—a nurse who has graduated from nursing school and received a nurse's license

INDEX

PHOTO CREDITS

Cameramann International, Ltd.—4 (top), 12 (left),
15, 19 (2 photos)

Gartman Agency:
  © Lee Balterman—26 (top)
  © Diana H. Olson—14 (left)

Journalism Services:
  © Paul E. Burd—16 (right)
  © Harry J. Przekop, Jr.—24, 28 (bottom)

© Emilie Lepthien—22

© Mike Leskiw—Cover, 4 (bottom), 6, (2 photos), 8,
16 (left), 23 (2 photos), 29 (right)

Nawrocki Stock Photo:
  © Michael Brohm—10 (3 photos), 25 (top), 26 (bot
  © Larry Brooks—17
  © Candee—28 (top), 29 (left)

Photri—12 (right), 14 (right), 20

Root Resources:
  © Dennis and Ilene MacDonald—25 (bottom)
  © Mary A. Root—13 (right)

Tom Stack and Associates:
  © Tom Stack—13 (left)
  © Don and Pat Valenti—9

ABOUT THE AUTHOR

JUNE BEHRENS has written more than fifty books, plays, and filmstrips for young people, touching on all subject areas of the school curriculum. Mrs. Behrens has for many years been an educator in one of California's largest public school·systems. She is a graduate of the University of California at Santa Barbara and has a Master's degree from the University of Southern California. Mrs. Behrens is listed in *Who's Who of American Women*. She is a recipient of the Distinguished Alumni Award from the University of California for her contributions in the field of education. She and her husband live in Rancho Palos Verdes, a southern California suburb.